GIVE UP SOMETHING BAD for LENT

GIVE UP SOMETHING BAD for LENT

A Lenten Study for Adults

JAMES W. MOORE

Abingdon Press
Nashville

GIVE UP SOMETHING BAD FOR LENT
A LENTEN STUDY FOR ADULTS
Copyright © 2012 by Abingdon Press

This book is printed on acid-free paper.

Library of Congress Cataloging-in-Publication Data

Moore, James W. (James Wendell), 1938-
  Give up something bad for Lent : an Lenten study for adults / James W. Moore.
    p. cm.
  ISBN 978-1-4267-5369-5 (pbk. : alk. paper) 1. Lent--Meditations. I. Title.
  BV85.M5755 2012
  263'.92--dc23

                                                    2012031232

Scripture quotations in this publication, unless otherwise indicated, are from the New Revised Standard Version of the Bible, copyright 1989, Division of Christian Education of the National Council of the Churches of Christ in the United States of America. Used by permission. All rights reserved.

12 13 14 15 16 17 18 19 20 21—10 9 8 7 6 5 4 3 2 1

MANUFACTURED IN THE UNITED STATES OF AMERICA

Contents

Introduction

For many years I did it, but no more . . . at least not in the same way. For years, like many other people, I gave up something for Lent as a spiritual discipline. On Ash Wednesday, the first day of the Lenten season, I would make a commitment to sacrificially give up something that was important to me as an exercise in self-denial. It was usually something I liked to eat such as desserts or hamburgers or pizza. One year I gave up ice cream. Another year it was soft drinks, and still another year it was coffee. One of the hardest was the Lenten season when I tried to give up chocolate. Was I ever glad to see Easter Sunday come that year!

But a few years ago, this all changed for me. I now go about this in a totally different way. That particular year, as Ash Wednesday approached and I began to think about what I would give up that year for Lent, all of a sudden out of the blue it hit me . . . a new idea! Why on earth had I not thought of this before?

I decided that if I am going to give up something for Lent, why not choose something bad? If I am going to sacrificially give up something for Lent as a spiritual discipline and as an exercise in self-denial, why not pick out something that I really need to get out of my life permanently? Instead of giving up desserts or hamburgers or chocolate, why not select something that spiritually I would be a whole lot better off without? Why not choose certain acts or certain attitudes or certain habits or certain sins that have the power to contaminate, infect, or poison my soul? Why not give up one of those for Lent? It's a good idea for all of us, isn't it? Why not intentionally decide, with the help of God, to put our energy and efforts into ridding ourselves of something that is destructive in our lives, something like envy or jealousy or self-pity or apathy or procrastination or gossip or resentment or blame-shifting or pettiness or negative thinking? Why not give up something bad for Lent in the hope and with the prayer that if we can give up that bad thing for the forty days of Lent this year then maybe, just maybe, God can give us the strength to give it up forever?

It is my genuine hope and prayer that as we go through the pages of this Lenten study and the accompanying Scripture lessons for each chapter together, we will be inspired and encouraged this year as never before to give up something bad for Lent and then be better prepared to wrap our arms around the good news of Easter.

Give Up Something Bad for Lent

Scripture: Read Matthew 5:29-30; 16:26

A few years ago, I was with some friends at a banquet in Texas. After a sumptuous meal, the waiters brought out a beautiful dessert. One man at our table said, "Oh, no! I can't even look at that!" "Why not?" we asked. He answered, "Because I'm giving up desserts for Lent, and I don't want to be tempted."

For years and years, people have given up something for Lent as a spiritual discipline, usually things like desserts, sweets, chocolate, coffee, tea, or ice cream. Some who are less disciplined will dramatically announce as a joke that they are giving up something that's out of season and not available like watermelon or strawberries, or something that they don't like anyway like spinach or Brussels sprouts. And others with tongue firmly in cheek will say they are giving up something they can't do anyway like space travel or running a four-minute mile.

Well, recently I've been thinking about this from another perspective. If we are going to give up something for Lent, instead of choosing something good, why not choose something bad? If we are going to give up something for Lent as a spiritual discipline, then why don't we pick out something that we really need to get out of our lives permanently? Why not give up something bad for Lent?

It happened one morning a few weeks before Easter in an adult Sunday school class. During the gathering-in time, people were drinking coffee and chatting informally. Suddenly someone asked, "What are you all giving up for Lent?" People began to discuss that question. Some took it very seriously and told what they were doing, but others took it very lightly. They joked, made wisecracks about it, and brushed the question aside. But then, one woman who had just gone through a painful divorce said something powerful. She said, "I've decided this Lent to give up being

unhappy! I'm going to give up being unhappy for Lent!"
That comment touched me deeply because it made a lot
of sense when I thought about it. After all, if we are going
to give up something for Lent as a spiritual discipline, why
not pick out something bad? Why not pick out something
that spiritually we would be a whole lot better off without?

It's really a very Biblical idea, isn't it? Jesus said to the
disciples that they should deny themselves, take up their
cross, and follow him (Matthew 16:24). And he says it to
us! Deny yourselves! Take up your cross! Follow me! We
also could say it this way: "Get rid of those things in your
life that prevent you from walking where Jesus would lead
you. Get rid of those things in your life that are not Christ-
like!" Then, Jesus put it even more graphically in the Sermon on the Mount. Listen to these shocking words: "If your
right eye causes you to sin, tear it out and throw it away; it
is better for you to lose one of your members than for your
whole body to be thrown into hell. And if your right hand
causes you to sin, cut it off and throw it away; it is better
for you to lose one of your members than for your whole
body to go into hell" (Matthew 5:29-30).

Tear it out? Cut it off? Throw it away? Did Jesus really say that? Is this the "gentle Jesus meek and mild"
who we sing about? Is this the personable Jesus who took
little children up into his arms and blessed them? Is this
the sensitive Jesus who loved the birds of the air and the

flowers of the field? Is this the compassionate Jesus who touched the man with the withered hand and made him whole? What are we to make of this? These words sound so harsh, so stark, so brutal. If your right hand offends you, cut it off.

There must be some truth here that is tremendously important to prompt Jesus to speak so strongly and so un-flinchingly. Obviously, Jesus is speaking symbolically here. He is not talking about acts involving knives and gouges. He means that anything that is destructive, anything that threatens to destroy us, and anything that seduces us to sin should be ruthlessly and radically cut out of our lives. Any part that threatens the existence of the whole must be eliminated before it contaminates and destroys.

If you are smoking and it's destroying your lungs, quit smoking. If you are drinking and you are becoming an alcoholic, quit drinking. If you are gambling and losing all your food money at the track, quit gambling. Whatever you are doing that is tainting and destroying your life, cut it off, quit it, and give it up before it does you in.

Although it sounds harsh and startling, the truth is that we do, as a matter of fact, operate on this "cut it off, give it up, get rid of it" principle all the time. Ask any doctor about this. If you have an appendix that is about to rup-ture and spread its poison into other parts of the body, the doctor will not hesitate to cut it out. If skin cancer appears on your finger and threatens to get into the bloodstream and spread to other parts of your body, the doctor will say, "Let's give it up." Ask any dentist, any athlete, or any singer, and they will all tell you that there are certain things that you have to give up before you can be your best.

Nowhere is this principle truer than in the spiritual dimension of our personal lives. There are certain acts, certain attitudes, certain habits, certain sins that will contaminate, infect, and poison our souls. The only way we can be spiritually well, spiritually fit, and spiritually whole is to get rid of them, give them up, cut them out. Nothing less than radical surgery will do!

Now, be honest with yourself and with God. What is in your life that you need to give up for Lent? What bad thing in your life right now do you need to get rid of? Let me list a few possibilities. I'm sure you will think of others.

FIRST, GIVE UP BITTERNESS.

Is there some bitterness in your life right now? If so, you had better give it up because it will poison your soul. Is there a grudge, a grievance, a smoldering hatred, a broken relationship that is tainting your life right now? If so, please don't go to sleep tonight until you have set it right.

The hit movie *Rain Man* is the story of a young man named Charlie Babbitt who became estranged from his father because of a confrontation that happened when Charlie was sixteen years old. Charlie brought home a good report card and wanted to take some of his buddies for a victory ride in his father's prized convertible. But his father said, "No!" Well, Charlie took the car anyway. His father had him arrested along with his buddies for stealing the car! The parents of the other boys bailed them out immediately, but to teach him a lesson, Charlie Babbitt's father left him in jail for two days! When Charlie finally got out of jail, he was so angry, so hurt, so hostile that he ran away from home.

Later, his father tried to contact him; but Charlie, still bitter, refused to respond. Finally, when Mr. Babbitt died, he left the convertible—the car that had caused their estrangement—to Charlie; and he left the remainder of his estate—over three million dollars—to Charlie's autistic brother named Raymond, a brother Charlie didn't even know he had.

As the story continues to unfold, Charlie is angry. He feels that he has lost his birthright to Raymond who is out of touch with reality, lives in a world all his own, and has absolutely no concept of the value of money. He thinks a candy bar and a sports car cost the same . . . about a hundred dollars!

Charlie Babbitt tries at first to use Raymond to get the money, but in the process he realizes that he really loves his brother and that's more important than the money. They connect in a wonderful way.

It's a beautiful story. It has some language in it that I wish they had left out, but it's a beautiful story. However, the story is tinged with sadness that is produced by seething bitterness. Look what Charlie missed over all those years, and I'm not talking about money. And look what Charlie's dad missed. All because of a festering unresolved bitterness.

Please don't let that happen to you. Remember how Jesus put it: "For what will it profit them if they gain the whole world but forfeit their life? Or what will they give in return for their life?" (Matthew 16:26). The King James Version translates the word for *life* as "soul." With every fiber of my being, I'm pleading with you to think about this. If there is bitterness in your life, give it up for Lent. Give it to God. Let God bring healing. With God's help, you can give it up forever!

SECOND, GIVE UP APATHY.

Apathy means quitting on life. Apathy means not caring. Apathy means not trying. It's amazing to me how many people there are in our world today who get discouraged and throw in the towel. If you want to give up something for Lent, give up apathy! Give up negative, cynical, pessimistic thinking.

I heard my college Bible teacher tell this story: Dr. Halford Luccock was a distinguished professor at Yale University a few years ago. He told a bittersweet story of his own youth. He and a few of his rebellious young friends decided to do something wicked, the wickedest thing they could think of. They decided to burn a Bible and not just any Bible. They slipped into Hal Luccock's father's study, took the huge book from the library, and set it on fire. But Mr. Luccock arrived on the scene unexpectedly and spoiled their fun by pointing out that the huge book the boys had burned was not the Bible at all but the dictionary, which of course contained exactly the same words but in a different arrangement. Then Mr. Luccock pointed out to the boys that we don't destroy words by burning them; we destroy them by not using them!

Burning the Bible is a wicked thing but ignoring the Bible is even worse. You see, we destroy good things by ignoring them. Churches, schools, families, marriages, friendships, commitments, physical health, spiritual life, intellectual growth: all these good things can be destroyed by neglect, by apathy. Apathy is the opposite of commitment, the opposite of faith, and it can ruin your life. If you want to give up something for Lent, why don't you pick out something bad to give up like bitterness or apathy?

FINALLY, GIVE UP DISCOURAGEMENT.

I heard a story about a preschool teacher who felt worn down and burnt out. She was a committed teacher, but she felt tired and discouraged. And the children were really beginning to get on her nerves. They were driving her up the wall. Then things got worse. Word came that her mother had died. She was very close to her mother, and she was devastated by her sudden loss.

After the funeral, she took some time off to work through her feelings. Her grief made it even harder for her to go back into the classroom. Finally, when she returned to school, she felt more like a soldier going into battle than a teacher of preschoolers. The first day back, she went through the motions like the competent professional she was. Even though she felt sorry for herself, she felt that she was covering it very well.

But on the second day back to school, something happened. She discovered five-year-old Rachel picking the last chrysanthemum from the flowerpot in the hall. Rachel, by the way, was the most distant, difficult, disruptive child in her class. In a stern, trembling voice, the teacher said, "Rachel, what are you doing?" Rachel held out in her little hand the flowers she had already picked. "Mrs. Terrell," she said, "You used to be like a mother. I know you are fussed in your mind. Maybe these flowers will help you be like a mother again."

Mrs. Terrell was taken back. *Fussed in my mind*, she thought. *You mean it shows? to a five-year-old?*

Then Mrs. Terrell asked, "Rachel, what is a mother like?"

"A mother is like you used to be," Rachel said.

"I like being with children. . . . It's just that, well, Rachel, my mother passed away and. . . ."

Rachel meekly interrupted, "You mean she died?"

"Yes, Rachel, she died."

Rachel looked up at her teacher with big brown eyes and asked, "Did your mother live until she died?"

Mrs. Terrell thought, *What kind of question is that?* "Well, honey, of course. All people live until they die. They . . ."

Rachel interrupted again, "Oh, no, they don't, Mrs. Terrell. Some people change. They stop being what they used to be. They walk around, but they don't seem alive anymore." Rachel paused, and then she said, "Please don't die, Mrs. Terrell. Stay alive for us. Be like a mother to us again."

Mrs. Terrell hugged her tightly and through tears she said, "I will Rachel! I will!"

All of us have moments when we get down, when we get discouraged, when we feel sorry for ourselves. All of us have to walk through difficult valleys. All of us have to experience the Good Fridays of life, but the good news is that Easter's coming. Easter's coming! And if during these days of Lent we can—with the help of God and by the grace of God—get rid of some of the bad things in our lives like bitterness, apathy, or discouragement, we will be better prepared to receive the Easter victory, the new life God has for us. And, if we can give up some of the things that are bad for us for Lent this year, then hopefully, prayerfully, we can give them up forever with the help of God.

Questions for Reflection and Discussion

1. What does Lent mean to you? Why is it important? What do you hope to receive from participating in this experience?

2. Why do you think people give up something for Lent? Have you ever given something up? What was it? What was the result?

3. What are some reasons to give up something bad for Lent? What might happen when we give it to God?

4. What dangers do you see in bitterness? Why do you think bitterness is often left unresolved?

5. Think about a time when you experienced apathy. What was it like? How can apathy harm your life?

6. When have you experienced discouragement? What are some ways to eliminate discouragement from your life?

Prayer

Dear God, thank you for the season of Lent. Remind us of the importance of preparing for and anticipating Easter. Help us to use this season wisely as we make positive changes in our lives. Amen.

Focus for the Week

Begin your observance of Lent by taking a personal inventory of your habits, strengths, and weaknesses. Look deep inside to see what is holding you back from a better relationship with God and others. Take the first steps toward giving up something bad for Lent.

Give Up Harsh, Condemning Judgments for Lent

Scripture: Read Matthew 7:1-5

Her name was Ellen. She was a junior in high school, an honor student, a member of the band, and secretary of her class. Her life was beautiful, her future bright; but then, everything went wrong. I was called on to conduct her funeral on what would have been her seventeenth birthday. It was suicide. In the depths of depression, she had taken an overdose of sleeping pills. She left a note saying that she couldn't go on. She couldn't fight the rumors and the rejection any longer. She felt betrayed by her friends and her community. It was all so sad, so useless, and such a waste. This tragic teenage suicide was sparked by a misunderstanding, by a false rumor, by people spreading vicious gossip, by ordinary people like you and me passing on a cruel, destructive untruth.

The rumor was that she had come home at daylight in a drunken stupor, her clothes disheveled, delivered to her door by an older man in a fancy sports car. That was the rumor. The truth was that she had sat up all night at the hospital with her gravely ill grandmother and had been brought home early the next morning by her uncle. That was the truth!

A neighbor saw something out her kitchen window and jumped to the wrong conclusions and then started spreading a false rumor. As a result, an innocent teenager was devastated. The harsh stares, the cruel jokes, the profane wisecracks, the vicious gossip, the whispering behind her back, the pointed fingers, and the blatant lies became too much for Ellen. Her fragile, sensitive personality couldn't take it. She cracked under the pressure, and in a moment of deep agony and excruciating emotional pain, she took her life. A young life with so much promise was snuffed out because people like you and me participated in spreading false rumors. When will we ever learn?

As far back as the Sermon on the Mount, Jesus warned us about this: "Do not judge, so that you may not be judged" (Matthew 7:1). This is not a suggestion, not a request, not a plea. It is a strong command, an emphatic order. Jesus is speaking straight from the shoulder here. He is not mincing words. He is not beating around the bush. He is coming on strong and giving us a stern warning: "Do not judge!"

Now, obviously Jesus knows that we have to make judgments, that we have to make decisions. We make hundreds of them every day: when we decide to get up rather than stay in bed, when we choose an oat bran breakfast, when we decide to stay home or go to church, when we select this book to read rather than the other, and when we opt to buy this rather than that, we are making judgments. We have to make value judgments and moral judgments. As a matter of fact, Jesus gave the Sermon on the Mount so that we might have insights and standards by which to make Christian decisions, Christian distinctions, and Christian judgments. Common sense tells us that we have to make those kinds of judgments constantly.

But, of course, these kinds of judgments are not what Jesus is talking about here in Matthew 7. If you look in the dictionary, you will find that the verb *judge* does indeed mean "to decide" or to "distinguish." In addition, it has another definition. *To judge* also means "to condemn" or "to censure." That's what Jesus is talking about here. In fact, that verse could be translated like this: "Condemn not, so that you be not condemned!" Our Lord is giving us a strong and forceful warning. "Judge not! Don't be so hard on people! Don't be so quick to criticize or censure others! Don't be so arrogantly self-righteous! Don't be so anxious to point the finger of guilt! Be gracious! Be kind! Judge not! Condemn not!"

Let me bring this closer to home by outlining for you some of the strong lessons of this verse in Matthew 7.

FIRST, AVOID MAKING HASTY, CONDEMNING JUDGMENTS BASED ON RUMOR.

Jesus' command "judge not" is a warning against making hasty, condemning judgments on the basis of rumor or hearsay. Beware of rumors! Jesus' warning is against gossip. This is the stuff that heartaches are made of. How often do we injure persons when we start or repeat a rumor or make a judgment without checking all the facts?

When I was a child, I learned a little rhyme that goes like this: "Sticks and stones may break my bones, but words will never hurt me!" One thing is wrong with this rhyme: It's not true! Words do hurt. Our worst hurts come not from sticks and stones, but from words. Words can rip us apart and knock the very life out of us. The pain we can cause, the hurt we can do with sharp, piercing, stinging words of rumor and hearsay and gossip is absolutely indescribable. Before we make our estimate of any event or any person, we need to wait. Wait on the facts. Wait on the truth. Wait on time.

When I was a young boy, most every Saturday I went to see the cowboy matinee movies at our community theater. It's amazing how often this mistake to rush to judgment was highlighted in those old Westerns. A stranger would come to town. Something bad would happen, and immediately the local citizens would point the finger at the new stranger in town as the likely culprit. The stranger would be arrested and put in jail to await a fair trial, which would come later when the traveling judge would ride over from Dodge City.

But the locals did not want to wait. They would become a lynch mob and march to the jail and demand that the sheriff hand over the stranger so they could have their justice immediately and purge their town of this evil stranger! But the sheriff and his deputy would stand on the porch of the jail with shotguns over their arms, and they would hold off the angry mob. The sheriff would say, "No! You cannot take justice into your own hands. We wait! The judge will be here in a couple of days, and we will have a fair trial for this accused man. Now go on home and wait for the trial!" Reluctantly, the crowd would disperse.

A few days later, the judge would arrive, and when the full truth would come out, the stranger would be proven innocent every time! And the point would be made. It is a dangerous thing to rush to judgment without all the facts. It is a dangerous thing to jump to conclusions without all of the information. It is a dangerous thing to make quick, hasty, condemning judgments based on rumor or hearsay.

Rotary International strongly advocates what they call "The Four-Way Test." It is excellent. It works like this: Before you say anything or pass anything on, you ask these four questions:

First, is it the *Truth*?

Second, is it *Fair* to all concerned?

Third, will it *Build Goodwill* and *Better Friendships*?

Fourth, will it be *Beneficial* to all concerned?[1]

If you can't answer these four questions with a firm yes, then don't say it! Jesus calls all of us to a gracious spirit when he says, "Judge not." He means first of all, "Beware of rumors."

SECOND, AVOID BEING UNKIND AND UNSYMPA-THETIC IN OUR JUDGMENTS.

Some years ago, when I first started out in the ministry, I served a church in a small town way out in the country. Now, we are talking small here! This little town had a grocery store, a service station, a feed store, a cotton gin, a church, a post office, a washateria, a school, a few hundred people, and that was about it. Every morning I had to walk over to the post office to get my mail, and every morning for two years, ol' Charley Smith would be sitting on the porch of the post office, whittling. Every morning as I walked by, he would cut his eyes toward me and say, "Nothin' against you yet, Preacher, nothin' against you yet!"

Now, that always filled me with an unsettling rush of mixed emotions! On the one hand, I was glad there was nothing against me. On the other hand, I knew they were looking for something. It was like two years of waiting for the other shoe to drop. Deep down in my soul, I longed for kindness, for compassion, for support. I wanted them to be kind and merciful and gracious in their judgment of me.

That's what we all want, isn't it? We are like the man named Sam who went in to have his picture made and said to the photographer, "Now, I want you to do me justice." The photographer took one look at Sam and said, "Sam, what you need is mercy, not justice!" That's what we all need. But so often we forget that, don't we? How easy it is to jump on the bandwagon and criticize other people harshly just because everyone's doing it? Strangely, bashing others has become something of a fad of our time. Politicians, personalities, groups, and even friends judge one another with hard words and merciless criticism. But then, we run upon the Sermon on the Mount, and Jesus brings us up short and says to us, "Judge not! Condemn not! Be gracious and merciful and compassionate." First, beware of false rumors. Second, beware of being unkind.

THIRD, OUR JUDGMENTS MAY BOOMERANG.

Beware of the boomerang effect! Our harsh judgments come back to haunt us. What we send out comes back. Over and over we see this in the Scriptures. The elder brother judges his prodigal brother harshly, and the elder brother is the one who misses the party and comes out looking bad (Luke 15:11-32). Martha judges her sister Mary harshly, and Martha ends up as the one who is embarrassed (Luke 10:38-42). That's the way it works, isn't it? Our harsh judgments boomerang on us. Thus the prayer: "Lord, make my words sweet and tender today for I may have to eat them tomorrow."

In his book *Look at the Burning Bushes*, Bishop Bob Goodrich writes about a schoolmaster some years ago who demanded strict discipline in his classroom. He required that all students must hold their textbooks in their left hands as they stood to recite. Early in the term, one young boy stood holding his book in his right hand. The teacher interrupted with a stern reminder that he should hold his textbook in his left hand. But the student continued with it in his right hand. The teacher exploded, shouting at him, "You take that book in your left hand right now or suffer the consequences!" "But, sir, I can't," said the boy. The teacher was so infuriated that he ran to the student screaming at the top of his voice, "Don't you disobey me!" Then he grabbed the boy and began to shake him and pushed him harshly down into his desk. Just then, an empty sleeve swung into view! The boy had no left arm, just an empty sleeve! The teacher was embarrassed, and he stammered out an apology.[2]

Two important lessons emerge from this dramatic story. First, everyone has an empty sleeve that we cannot see, and if we knew about it, we would be more understanding and less critical. We need to be more sensitive to the empty sleeves hidden away in the lives of people. Second, our hard, condemning judgments boomerang. They come back to haunt us. They reveal far more about us than they reveal about the one we are judging.

ONE FINAL THOUGHT: JUDGMENT BELONGS TO GOD.

When Jesus says, "Do not judge," he is reminding us that judgment belongs to God and not to us. Judgment belongs to God, and thank God for that. It means that ultimately we are to be judged not by other people, but by the one who knows us and understands us and loves us, by the one who knows the whole truth about us, by the one who knows all about the empty sleeves in our lives.

If we could—by the grace of God—give up harsh, condemning judgments of others for Lent this year, hopefully, prayerfully, we can give up this bad and hurtful practice forever.

Questions for Reflection and Discussion

1. What stories do you know about the ways rumors have hurt people? What are some of the ways that rumors start? What are some of the dangers of spreading gossip?

2. Why do you think Jesus gives us such a strong warning against judging others?

3. How do you respond to the four questions that the Rotary Club gives as a guide for judging whether or not to pass along information? If everyone asked these questions, how might our culture and our world be different?

4. Think about a time you were either on the giving or receiving end of an unkind remark. How did it feel? What did you think? What happened as a result of the unkind remark?

5. What are some examples of how judgments may boomerang? What are some of the consequences?

6. Why do you think we should leave judgment of others to God and God alone?

Prayer

Dear God, thank you for reminding us about the dangers of rumors and gossip. Help us to refrain from judgment and explain the actions of others in the kindest way. May we treat others the way we wish to be treated. Amen.

Focus for the Week

This week, focus on watching what you say about others. Remember that silence is often golden. Offer encouragement and kind words when possible. Practice giving sympathy to others this week. Start a new habit of sharing good news.

1. From *http://www.rotary.org/en/aboutus/rotaryinternational/guidingprinciples/pages/ridefault.aspx*.
2. From *Look at the Burning Bushes*, by Robert E. Goodrich, Jr. (Spiritual Life Publishers, 1963); pages 61-62.

Give Up the Enemies Within for Lent

Scripture: Read Luke 11:37-52

Her name is Johnnie. A few years ago, she was driving her automobile through the streets of her hometown. She was on her way to a routine doctor's appointment. But as she turned right onto one of the main streets of town, a small four-year-old girl named Tracey ran out in front of Johnnie's car without warning. Careful driver that she was, Johnnie saw her immediately. She hit the brakes and the horn and tried to swerve left to miss her, but it was too late! As Johnnie's vehicle came to a screeching halt, little Tracey was struck by the front of the car and sucked up underneath it. At the time of the impact, Tracey was hugging her new stuffed teddy bear to her chest, and the major blow was taken by the teddy bear.

Horrified by what had happened, Johnnie jumped out of the driver's seat and ran to the front of the car. She knelt down and saw Tracey pinned underneath. The bottom part of the engine was pressing down on the little girl's chest, but the teddy bear was cushioning the pressure some-what. Tracey was conscious, alert, and moving her arms and legs. Johnnie screamed for help. As people ran to her aid, Johnnie did an unbelievable thing. She put her hands under the front bumper of the car, lifted it up, and held it some six inches off the ground so that Tracey could be pulled out to safety. Tracey was rushed to the hospital and shortly thereafter was released with only minor scrapes and bruises thanks to her teddy bear and to the heroic efforts of Johnnie. Now, Johnnie is not a weightlifter, not an athlete, not a person of super-strength. Actually she is rather small in physical stature, but in that moment of crisis, she lifted the front end of a 3,000-pound car to save the life of a little girl.

Later, when Johnnie went on to her doctor's appoint-ment, the doctor found that she had strained some mus-cles in her shoulders and legs from lifting the car, but other than those minor problems, she was in excellent shape. By the way, the baby Johnnie gave birth to three months later was just fine too! Isn't that something? A young expectant mother (six months pregnant) somehow in that moment of crisis found deep down inside of her an incredible strength to do the impossible. I'm sure that adrenaline made it possible, but I think there was something more.

I think that we all have astonishing strengths and powers and capabilities deep within us that we have not begun to tap. Now, put that over against the horrifying news stories that came out of Matamoros, Mexico, in 1989. In the name of Satanism, voodoo, cult worship, bizarre beliefs, superstitions, and drug trafficking, many innocent people were brutalized, mutilated, and ritually sacrificed at the command of a Cuban godfather who told his followers that the killings would bring them protection from their enemies.[1] One suspect—after confessing that he shot one victim and decapitated another—said, "We killed them for our protection." All of this horrendous activity was directly related to an illegal drug operation.[2]

How do these two radically different news stories relate to one another? The point is that we as human beings have incredible powers and amazing capabilities within us, which when properly harnessed and used can enable us to do astonishing God-like things; but when those powers within us become corrupted or contaminated, they can cause us to do dreadful, evil, horrible, despicable things. Those powers within us, when rightly motivated, can save lives; if wrongly motivated, they devastate and kill. In Matamoros, when many spectators saw the suspects in custody they commented that the suspects looked so normal. Yet they did those horrifying, brutal things. This is yet another dramatic reminder that outward appearances can be deceiving. It's what's inside that counts.

That's what Luke 11 is all about. Jesus is reminding us here that the inner life is so important. That's where the major battles are won or lost.

Luke 11:37-41 underscores the importance of the inner life and the need we all have for inner cleansing. In the Gospel of Matthew (5:1-12), we have the Beatitudes that begin with the words "Blessed are. . . ." In Luke 11:42-52, the coin is turned over. Instead of blessings, we find six woes expressed against some of the Pharisees and lawyers.

Jesus has finished speaking and a Pharisee who has been there in the crowd listening to him invites him to dinner. Jesus goes home with him, sits down at his table, and begins to eat without the ritual of washing his hands before dinner. The Pharisee is astonished by this. Jesus senses his displeasure and says, "Now you Pharisees clean the outside of the cup and of the dish, but inside you are full of greed and wickedness. You fools! Did not the one who made the outside make the inside also? So give for alms those things that are within; and see, everything will be clean for you" (verses 39-41).

The key that unlocks what this is all about is the last sentence. It simply means that if all things within you are done in love, then automatically everything else will be clean as well. I don't know if you noticed this or not, but this is not much of a conversation. It's pretty one-sided. The Pharisee may not have uttered a word. That, I guess, is what is happening here. The Pharisee doesn't speak, but his body language makes it abundantly clear that he is disgusted because Jesus did not wash his hands before the meal. He had neglected the ceremonial hand washing. It would be a little bit like inviting the preacher home for Sunday dinner and seeing him dive right in and start eating without saying grace.

Jesus responds with this by talking about the outside and the inside of the cup and the plate, and he tells the Pharisee that it is not consistent to be worried about external cleansing when inwardly you are filled with wickedness and greed. These are strong words. Jesus was, without question, tremendously concerned about what's going on inside of people. He was greatly concerned about the inner life. He knew that it's not enough to be outwardly clean. It's not enough to talk a good game. It's not enough to go through the motions.

A few years ago, a barbers' supply association had a convention in Chicago. As a publicity stunt they went out to Skid Row and found a man lying in the gutter, filthy dirty and filthy drunk. They brought him back to the convention center. They cleaned him up, shampooed him, shaved him, put cologne on him, and washed him with a new kind of soap they were trying to sell. They bought him a new suit, shirt, tie, and shoes; and they said to all the world, "This is what our barber supplies can do for you." But the next day when they looked for him again, they found him right back in Skid Row, lying in the gutter, filthy and drunk. The point is clear. It's just not enough to clean someone up on the outside. It's what's inside that really counts. God works from the inside out, and that's where the real cleansing has to take place.

Let's bring this closer to home. Let's look together at some of the enemies within, at some of the pressures, tensions, or temptations within us that—if left unchecked— can drag us to a level of life not in keeping with the image of God. Of course, there are many things we could list here such as pride, greed, hatred, jealousy, hostility, laziness, and lust; but for now, look with me at three of the most deceptive and subtle enemies within.

FIRST OF ALL, ENVY

Envy is so sneaky, so tricky. It is one of the most dangerous enemies within, and it is most likely to appear in full strength with people who are our competitors (either overtly or covertly) and when there is a limited amount of room at the top. For example, a lawyer isn't likely to be upset if someone says to him, "Dr. X is the best surgeon in town." But if you tell him that Mr. Y is the best lawyer in town, envy may begin to perk up unless he is careful. It's in our own field, against our own competitors, that envy can pervade our spirits and poison our souls. This is probably why Jesus was so upset at some of the religious leaders of his day. They saw him as a competitor. They saw him attracting the people. They saw him winning in their field of expertise, and they couldn't stand it. Envy took control and pulled them down to a level of life that became dangerous, destructive, and sinful, that caused the Son of God to be nailed to a cross.

We are still doing it—not as graphically as what happened at Golgotha, not as despicably as what happened at Matamoros—but we are still doing it. We crucify people with words and attitudes. We destroy people with gossip and pointing fingers. Duped by the deceptive way envy takes control, we then try to justify our actions by saying, "It was the right thing to do. We had to do it for our own protection. We had to do it for the common good." When will we ever learn? Envy is so dangerous. Envy is an enemy within. Envy is an enemy of God. It can get people crucified, and it can devastate our souls.

SECOND, BLAME-SHIFTING

Blame-shifting is the temptation to rationalize, to explain away, to point the finger at someone else to get the attention off of us. It is an enemy within that the Bible exposes repeatedly. In Genesis 3, the man and woman eat the forbidden fruit. The man blames both God and the woman: "The woman whom you gave to be with me, she gave me the fruit from the tree, and I ate." The woman blames the serpent: "The serpent tricked me, and I ate" (3:12-13). Later, in Exodus, when things get tough in the desert, the people turn on Moses and blame him for their hunger. "If only we had died by the hand of the LORD in the land of Egypt, when we sat by the fleshpots and ate our fill of bread; for you have brought us out into this wilderness to kill this whole assembly with hunger" (16:3). In other words, "You're the one to blame, Moses. You brought us out here to die in the wilderness. Why didn't you just leave us alone in Egypt?" Then in the New Testament, we see Pontius Pilate trying to pass the buck and shift the blame (Matthew 27:11-26).

We all do it, don't we? It's an ever-present temptation. The boss blames his secretary. She blames a co-worker. The co-worker goes home and kicks the dog. Someone put it like this: "The trouble with some people is that they won't admit their faults. I'd be the first to admit mine if I had any." It's a favorite ploy of little children and immature grown-ups to shift the blame. "She told me to." "I couldn't help it." "Everybody else was doing it." "He started it when he hit me back." "The devil made me do it." One of the first things our son Jeff learned to say was a neat cover-up when he knew he had done something wrong. "It's O.K., Dad," he would say. "We'll tell Mom you did it." Some of these kinds of rationalizations can be cute in little children, but they are sad, pitiful, and tragic in adults.

Blaming things on others or on Satan is a cop-out. Demonic powers, witches, black magic, or superstition do not control us. God gave us freedom to choose. We don't need a scapegoat. We have a savior. Envy and blame-shifting are enemies within.

FINALLY, SELF-PITY

A few weeks ago, I was really down. I felt physically tired, emotionally drained, mentally exhausted, and I couldn't figure out why. Then I realized what it was: I was feeling sorry for myself. I was nursing a hurt. Someone had said something to me that cut like a knife. Some years ago when our daughter Jodi was two or three years old, when things weren't going her way she would sometimes say, "You hurt ALL my feelings!" Well, that's the way I was feeling. All my feelings were hurt, and I realized that I was giving in to self-pity.

Let me tell you something. Self-pity can ruin our lives. It depletes us physically, mentally, emotionally, and spiritually. It's an enemy within that can cut us off from God and from people. The good news of our faith is that God loves us and accepts us. No matter how others may treat us, God never deserts us or forsakes us. God is always there for us, and when we feel alone or rejected or hurt, we need to remember that.

When we remember God's love, and when we pass that love on to others, then we can—with the help of God, by the grace of God—rise above envy and blame-shifting and self-pity. With God's strength and power, we can be victorious over the enemies within. And if we can give up these enemies within for Lent this year, hopefully, prayerfully, it can be the first step in giving them up forever.

Questions for Reflection and Discussion

1. What does the phrase "enemies within" suggest to you? What images, feelings, or thoughts come to mind?

2. Read Luke 11:37-52. Why do you think Jesus places such emphasis on the inner life? What does the inner life suggest to you? What does it mean to say that God works from the inside out?

3. How do you think we become victims of envy? Why is envy so dangerous?

4. What are some of the reasons people engage in blame-shifting?

5. Think about a time when you experienced self-pity. What was it like? In what ways can self-pity be destructive?

6. What is an "enemy within" that you would like to give up for Lent? What might be different in your life if you gave it up permanently?

Prayer

Dear God, thank you for opening our eyes to the enemies around us, especially our enemies within. Help us to look inside ourselves and replace our enemies with love, hope, and faith. Show us the way to make this Lent a beginning of positive change in our lives and the lives of others. Amen.

Focus for the Week

This week, identify and engage inner enemies in battle. Replace destructive habits with positive ones. Ask God to help you change your behaviors this Lent. Begin taking small steps toward a better you.

1. From *http://articles.latimes.com/1989-05-07/news/mn-3487_1_cult-mexico-city-mexico-s-federal-district.*
2. From *http://www.nytimes.com/1989/04/13/us/drugs-death-and-the-occult-meet-in-grisly-inquiry-at-mexico-border.html.*

Give Up Running Away for Lent

Scripture: Read Luke 9:10-17

Some years ago, a minister in Lubbock, Texas, told of a strange idea he had as a little boy. He thought that he could outrun germs. He once came down with a terrible cold, and he got the idea that if he could run fast from one room to another, he could get away from those germs the way he could get away from his puppy if he ran fast enough. His mother found him dashing from room to room all out of breath, and when she discovered what he was attempting to do, she gently but wisely called him back to reality. She explained that he couldn't outrun the germs. No matter where or how fast he went, the germs would go with him. "The sooner you quit trying to run away from your cold and start doing what the doctor prescribed, the quicker you will get well," she said.

The story holds a great truth for dealing with all of life's problems. We can't outrun our problems. The sooner we accept this fact and decide to face them, the better; but often we are slow to understand and practice this truth. We engage in an incessant search for a way to escape the inescapable, the chronic resentment associated with our problems. In doing so, we waste an incredible amount of our energy. We squander a large portion of our lives running, hiding, fleeing, and escaping.

If we look thoughtfully at our culture, we may be tempted to think of our time as an age of escapism. The reference may be appropriate. Look at what is happening. For example, we see an increase in drug abuse. While we know about the physical realities of addiction and the distorted ideas about what it means to have fun, we may ask, Why do people begin to use and abuse drugs? In many cases it has to do with escape. Some use drugs to get high or to get above and beyond their problems, but they ultimately crash. The result is that they often have more trouble than they started with in the first place. Some may take drugs so they can sleep because if they can sleep then they can avoid their problems at least for a little while. When they wake up, however, the problems are still there. Some take drugs so they can relax. They hope that somehow the tension might be released or eased, but the tension returns. The nerves stretch tighter, and sometimes they snap. Some use drugs such as alcohol in order to get drunk so they can forget their problems. When they sober up, the troubles are still there, often along with a terrible hangover. Some people take drugs so they can cope with life's problems. They believe that a pill will make them brave, calm them down, give them strength, or settle their nerves.

All of these abuses and misuses of drugs are simply our childish attempts to outrun the germs, our infantile ways of trying to run away from or hide from our problems. When will we ever learn that there is no escape from the problems of this world?

PROBLEMS ARE HERE TO STAY.

Ours is not a problem-free world. The world in which we live has no problem-free jobs, no problem-free marriages, no problem-free homes, no problem-free communities, no problem-free churches. We can't run away or escape. We have to face the problems, handle the difficulties, and deal with the troubles. We have no hiding place. We have no place to run.

We need to learn how to cope with our hardships creatively, productively, and meaningfully. Once again, our great teacher is Jesus. We see in him the model and the pattern for dealing with problems productively. His life and ministry demonstrate how we can cope with difficulties in creative ways.

We see his example in one of the most famous events in his life—the time when he fed the five thousand in the wilderness. This episode must have made a deep impression on the disciples because it is recorded in all four of the Gospels.[1] The story was familiar to me when I looked at it again this week, but I was amazed to discover just how relevant it is to this particular issue of coping with life's difficulties. This story depicts Jesus up against a real down-to-earth problem, and the way he responded is fascinating and enlightening.

At this time, Jesus and his disciples were trying to get away by themselves so they could reflect on the mission the twelve had just completed. They were "getting away" not "running away," and there's a big difference. They went to the city of Bethsaida. But the people followed them! One of the great things about Jesus was that he never looked on needy human beings as a nuisance. Instead, out of deep compassion, he rearranged his plans and worked with these interruptions constantly and meaningfully (verses 10-11).

Now, his disciples were more like us. They weren't so patient or understanding. They weren't so compassionate or gracious or generous or creative. I suspect that they were worn out, that they had had it with the crowd, and that they wanted to be rid of them. They realized that the people were hungry and tired. Crowds in this condition could get hostile and out of hand. So they began to strategize. They pulled Jesus aside and pointed out the difficulty and suggested, "Send the crowd away, so that they may go into the surrounding villages and countryside, to lodge and get provisions; for we are here in a deserted place" (verse 12). It was a perfectly natural suggestion in the face of what Jesus and the disciples were facing: a problem situation, one that was full of stress and potential danger.

Notice how Jesus dealt with the problem. His response is a beautiful model for us that shows creative ways to cope with problems. It can be outlined in three stages: (1) He chose to cope rather than run. (2) He used the available resources. (3) He turned the problem into an opportunity.

FIRST, JESUS CHOSE TO COPE RATHER THAN RUN.

Jesus chose to face the problem rather than flee from it. He refused to follow the disciples' suggestion that they employ the strategy of "escapism." He decided instead to face the situation squarely and openly and confidently, trusting God to help bring him through it. Instead of saying, "Trouble is coming; let's go our way and let them go theirs," he said in essence, "We are involved in this event together. We cannot pass the buck. Let's face it and deal with it." Then with the help of God, Jesus fed them.

It is clear from this response that for Jesus, the way out was to take the way through the situation. To him, the solution to the problem could not be found through running or hiding but through facing it squarely, facing it head-on, facing it directly and courageously, facing it with trust in God. That's the first thing we find here—Jesus chose to cope rather than run. Now here is a second key to coping with life's problems.

SECOND, JESUS USED AVAILABLE RESOURCES.

Jesus surveyed what resources were available, and he used them to solve the problem. Sometimes we fail to do this. The problem looms so large and seems so formidable that our minds are closed. We suffer from tunnel vision, and as a result, we cannot see the resources, tools, and opportunities that are available to help us.

Several years ago, I saw Robert Redford's film *The Natural*, an adaptation of a novel by Bernard Malamud. One man I know said it was the perfect movie for him and his wife because he loves baseball and she loves Robert Redford! In *The*

Natural, Robert Redford portrays an outstanding baseball player named Roy Hobbs who is a naturally gifted athlete. In his early twenties, he is on his way to try out with the Chicago Cubs when he meets with misfortune and mysteriously disappears for fifteen or sixteen years. Then, he shows up to play baseball for a major league team called the New York Knights. At the age of thirty-four, he walks into the dugout with a five hundred dollar contract in his hand and reports to the manager, a crusty old baseball character named Pop Fisher.

Pop thinks it's a joke. The Knights players laugh and snicker at this thirty-four-year-old rookie named Roy Hobbs. This is unheard of; Rookies are nineteen, twenty, twenty-one, not thirty-four! This is the age you retire from baseball, not when you start. Pop tries to get rid of him, but Roy Hobbs won't leave. He has a contract. So they give him a uniform and put him on the bench.

Day after day, the New York Knights baseball team plays terribly. They get worse and worse. They can't hit, they can't field, they can't score, and they drop lower and lower in the standings. The Knights are in a dire financial situation, and their only hope is to win the pennant. Pop is frustrated, worried, and scared. He does not realize that he has a great baseball player sitting on the bench. Finally, the Knights give Roy Hobbs a chance. They let him take batting practice. They throw his five pitches, and Hobbs hits all five out of the park! Finally, Pop sees this available resource, and he puts Roy Hobbs in the lineup. Hobbs inspires the other players with his great play, and they begin to win. And they keep on winning! And they win the pennant. The movie has a happy ending, and I love happy endings!

The point is that Pop made the mistake we often make. He didn't realize the available resource he had right there under his nose in the dugout. We often do that. We get so blinded by the enormity or complexity of the problems that we don't see and use the resources right at our fingertips.

I remember a story about another unrecognized resource. Some years ago in a small Mississippi Delta town, a man was driving a small foreign car when the back right wheel came off. When the wheel came off, it broke all four of the lug bolts that attach the wheel to the car. The man had a big problem. There were no lug bolts in that small town that he could buy. The closest parts store was twenty miles away. What in the world could he do? The police, the fire department, the mayor, even the men playing check- ers on the court square gathered around the car, but no one could figure out what to do.

Then along came Crazy Leroy. He was the town char- acter. They called him Crazy Leroy because he sometimes did bizarre things and often didn't appear to be very bright. The men decided to tease Crazy Leroy, so they brought him over and showed him the car, the wheel, and the broken lug bolts. They asked him what he would do if it were his car. "Very simple," said Crazy Leroy. "The other three wheels have four lug bolts. I would take one off each wheel, and use those three to attach this wheel, and then I would drive to Jackson and buy four new lug bolts." The crowd was amazed and cheered for Crazy Leroy, and then they asked him how he figured that out. Crazy Leroy replied, "I may be a little crazy, but I'm not dumb."

It's amazing what you can do if you just use the available resources. Jesus found out quickly that they had five loaves and two fish. He took what they had and used it to the best of his ability. He trusted God. God took the little and made it enough, and God made it work. When we trust God and use what we have to the best of our ability, God takes our little, makes it enough, and makes it work.

FINALLY, JESUS TURNED THE PROBLEM INTO AN OPPORTUNITY.

With the power of God, Jesus turned what looked like a defeat into a victory. He turned a burden into a blessing. We can do the same.

Years ago, Bishop Goodrich told the story of the noted German author Schiller's beautiful children's story. It was the legend of how birds got their wings. According to the legend, at first the little birds didn't have wings. They just scampered about on the ground. But one day, God got worried about them. So that night while they were asleep, God attached wings to their sides. The next morning when the little birds woke up, they felt so burdened by these heavy, cumbersome things attached to their sides. It was a problem for them to move about. Those wings were such a nuisance. They complained and fussed and felt sorry for themselves. But then some of the birds began to move the wings, and they were surprised at how graceful it felt. Suddenly, some of them began to fly. Then others began to move their wings, and they flew also. Now, the point of the legend is obvious, and it offers a beautiful lesson for life. What seemed at first to be a heavy, great burden to the little birds became their means of flight, the means by which they could soar into the skies.

Our problems can become opportunities. Our problems can become the means by which we soar into a higher level of living, a higher level of maturity, and a higher level of faith. With the help of God, we can give up running away not just for Lent this year, but forever.

Questions for Reflection and Discussion

1. What does running away bring to mind for you? When have you tried to run away from a problem? What was the result?

2. What are some of the ways that people "escape"? When is escapism helpful? When is it harmful?

3. Read Luke 9:10-17. How do you respond to the disciples' suggestions? What challenges you or inspires you about Jesus' ways of dealing with the hungry crowd?

4. What do you see as benefits of coping with a problem rather than running away from it?

5. When did you discover resources you had previously overlooked? What were the resources? How were you able to use them to solve a problem? How do you think God was present?

6. What are some of the "wings" or cumbersome things in your life that ultimately helped you to fly? What do these experiences say to you about turning problems into opportunities?

Prayer

Dear God, thank you for giving us the wisdom and courage to face our problems and not run away from them. Help us to deal with problems productively and to help others do the same. Remind us that you are always just a prayer away and eager to advise us on how to solve our problems. Amen.

Focus for the Week

This week, practice putting your problems on the run rather than running from your problems. Enlist God and others to help you conquer obstacles you face. Trust God for positive outcomes. Pray that you can banish fear.

1. From *The New Interpreter's Bible,* Volume IX (Abingdon Press, 1995); page 195.

Give Up a Bad Habit for Lent

Scripture: Read Luke 19:1-10

Recently, I gave my family a new book. The gesture on my part was a bit like the little boy who gave his mother a skateboard for her birthday or his grandfather a package of bubble gum, hoping he will get to share in the gift. I gave the book to my family hoping they would let me read it, and they have. The book is entitled *Happiness is Sharing*. It's a collection of thoughts on the meaning of happiness including thoughts written down by some world-famous people like

Albert Schweitzer, Helen Keller, Rose Kennedy, Dick Van Dyke, Pablo Casals, and many others.

One night last week, I ran across a fascinating article in the book. J. Harvey Howells wrote it, and in it he tells of a wonderful bedtime ritual he observes with his children, a ritual that has become a nightly habit for all the members of the family. I found this intriguing. Look at his words:

'You forgot something,' said my six-year-old urgently as I bent to kiss him good night. He grabbed my hand. 'You forgot to ask me what was the happiest thing that happened today.' 'I'm sorry. So I did.' I sat down on the edge of the bed. At last came the whisper. 'Catching that sand eel.' A contented sigh. 'My first fish.' He snuggled into the pillow. 'Night, Dad.'

When it started I do not know. Nor do I know how, but this prayerlike ritual has been my own private blessing since beyond memory. There is a moment of complete loneliness that comes to everyone every day. When the last good night has been murmured and the head is on the pillow, the soul is utterly alone with its thoughts. It is then that I ask myself, 'What was the happiest thing that happened today?'

The waking hours may have been filled with stress and even distress; I have been in a highly competitive business all my life. But no matter what kind of day it has been, there is always a 'happiest' thing. Funnily enough, it's rarely a big thing. Mostly it's fleeting loveliness. Waking to the honk of Canada geese on a crisp fall morning. An unexpected letter from a friend who doesn't write often. A cool swim on a broiling day. Listening to 'Seventy-six Trombones.' Camellias in the snow in an amazed New Orleans. My wife's face when she makes me laugh. There's always something, and as result I have never had a sleeping pill in my life. I doubt if my son will ever need one either—if he, too, remembers that happiness is not a goal dependent on some future event. It is with us every day if we make [cultivate the *habit*] the conscious effort to recognize it.[1]

I like Howells' article because there is great truth in it, and it shows us the power of a good habit.

Jesus knew about the power in good habits. As a matter of fact, in the Sermon on the Mount in Matthew 5 in the section we call the Beatitudes, Jesus is really saying to us, "Cultivate these good habits in your life. Cultivate humility, compassion, mercy, righteousness, peace-making. Cultivate these good habits, and you will discover true happiness." You see, the power of a good habit is something extra special, and Jesus knew it. We also know that bad habits are destructive. They can rip us apart, devastate us, demoralize us, and choke the very life out of us.

Luke 19:1-10 tells the story of the encounter between Jesus and Zacchaeus, "a chief tax collector" (verse 2). Tax collectors worked for the Roman government, and they had the power to collect extra taxes in order to make a profit.[2] Zacchaeus was rich (verse 2). Bad habits took root in him, took control of him, imprisoned him. The habits of greed, selfishness, and avarice had possessed him, cutting him off from other people and from God. Luke tells us that "[Zacchaeus] was trying to see who Jesus was" (verse 3). But then, Jesus saw him! And Jesus went to Zacchaeus' house for dinner! The encounter changed his life. We see in his experience the drama of redemption that led Zacchaeus to change his bad habits.

In Zacchaeus, we see vividly how we can change our habits and change our lives. We see here how we can, with God's help, break the curse of a bad habit. We see four specific steps that really work:

Step one: Recognize your bad habit and call it by name.
Step two: Make up your mind to stop it now.
Step three: Replace your bad habit with a good habit.
Step four: Realize that you have an outside source of strength.

Let's walk through these together.

STEP ONE: RECOGNIZE YOUR BAD HABIT AND CALL IT BY NAME.

Be specific. Don't whitewash it. Call it what it is. Be honest with yourself even if the truth hurts. This is the first step in overcoming a bad habit. Let me show you what I mean.

Some years ago when we were living in Tennessee, I went to visit a man in jail. He was charged with stealing thousands of dollars from the bank in which he had worked for more than twenty years. Embezzlement of bank funds, they called it. He looked clean-cut and seemed totally out of place behind bars. Before his arrest, he was one of the most beloved workers in the bank and one of the most respected men in the community.

The embezzlement had all started so innocently. One day after closing hours, a woman came to put some money in the bank. The man, a bank official who was the only worker there at the time, tried to explain that the books were already closed for the day and the vault was locked. But the woman insisted. So the man took her money and took it home with him in his suit pocket, fully intending to bring it back the next day. However, he forgot about it, and the next day he had to juggle the books a bit to cover his oversight. Then he told himself that since it was done, he would wait another day before turning the money in. Finally, he told himself that he was really underpaid and that he needed the money more than the bank, so he kept it.

Soon it happened again. He took some more money home. And then it happened again and again and again. It got easier each time, until soon, he had so rationalized it that he took money home with him every night. Before long, he had taken thousands and thousands of dollars.

Our sins have a way of finding us out, however. He was caught, arrested, put in jail, and was now facing criminal charges of embezzlement. I'll never forget what he said to me. He said, "I never thought of myself as a thief. When they started using words like *robber, stealer, embezzler, criminal* to describe me, I was shocked; I couldn't believe they were talking about me. I had deluded myself with my own rationalizations. I was blinded by my own bad habits, and I couldn't even see what was happening and what I had become." His words dramatically reveal the first step in overcoming a bad habit. We must honestly recognize it, see it, and call it by name.

This is what happened to Zacchaeus. Jesus got his attention and turned him around. Somehow the presence of Jesus, the goodness of Jesus, the light of Jesus, exposed the bad habits of Zacchaeus.

I had a teacher in college who was always so neat, so clean, so immaculate, that every time I stood beside her, I felt unkempt and rumpled. I found myself wishing that my clothes were a little neater and that my shoes were shined a little better. Jesus affected people like that spiritually. His goodness and his cleanness exposed "spiritual tackiness." Maybe this is what happened to Zacchaeus. When Jesus came into his life, he saw himself as he really was. Maybe before he saw Jesus he had rationalized his actions, but in the presence of Christ his rationalizations seemed weak and flimsy. Maybe he wondered how he could have been so blind. In the presence of Jesus, he saw himself as a traitor to God and to his people. He saw himself as one who had gotten rich at the expense of others. He saw himself as one who had "sold out." He saw how selfish and greedy he had been, and he didn't like what he saw.

Here is the point. The first step in breaking the curse of a bad habit is to see the bad habit for what it really is, recognize it, hold it up, look at it under the light of Christ, and call it by name! Don't whitewash it or explain it or rationalize it away. See it for what it really is. That's the first step.

STEP TWO: MAKE UP YOUR MIND TO STOP IT NOW.

If you want to get rid of a bad habit, you must make up your mind to stop it now. Habits are strange because they are often formed subtly and gradually, but often they have to be stopped "cold turkey"—abruptly and immediately. I have never known anyone who set out to become an alcoholic, only a person who took the first drink and then another and another until finally the habit was established. I've never known a single person who set out to be a liar. But one falsehood started the habit pattern and then another was told and another and the pattern became established. And so it goes. A habit begins with a single decision. We decide to do a thing, and that decision makes it likely that we will make the same decision in the future. First, we do a thing because we want to. Then we do it because we did it before. At last, we do it because we can't help it.

It all begins with a choice, and it must end with a choice. We must make up our minds to stop it now! I'm not so sure it can be gradual. Sometimes a radical break is necessary. It's not enough to say, "I won't tell as many lies today as I did yesterday." No! We have to say, "I will not be a liar anymore!" A woman once asked her minister, Dr. Brooks, "How early shall I teach my child religious habits?" Dr. Brooks said, "How old is your child?" She said, "Three." Her minister responded, "Hurry home, woman! Hurry home! You are four years late already!"

That day in Jericho, Zacchaeus must have realized that "time was a-wasting," so he made up his mind to stop his bad habits right then. He came down out of that sycamore tree, spent time with Jesus, and made a commitment to change and to do better. Today! Right now! To break the curse of a bad habit, we have to first recognize it and call it by name; second, we have to make up our minds to stop it right now.

STEP THREE: REPLACE YOUR BAD HABIT WITH A GOOD ONE.

Not long ago, I was visiting in a home in southwest Houston. I was sitting in the den of this fashionable home talking with the young mother who lived there. Her baby, who was just a few months old, was playing on the floor behind her. I could not believe my eyes when I saw the baby reach under the sofa and grab an old much-gnawed-upon dog's bone. You know what the baby did? He began chewing on the bone! Now, let me ask you something: How do you tactfully tell a young mother that her baby is chewing on a dog's bone? After a few moments, I called it to her attention, and she did a very smart thing. She took the bone away from her baby, but wisely, in the same motion, she replaced it with a nice, clean new teething ring. The baby never missed a chomp.

You see, we can't just take something away or we leave behind a vacuum. We have to replace the bad with something good. Again, we see it in Zacchaeus. He had been consumed with the habit of greed, but when he came down from that sycamore tree and spent time with Jesus, he began thinking of others: "Look, half of my possessions, Lord, I will give to the poor; and if I have defrauded anyone of anything, I will pay back four times as much" (verse 8). Greed had been taken away. Generosity had been put in its place. This is essential to getting rid of a bad habit. We have to call it by name, make up our mind to stop it, and replace the bad habit with a good one.

STEP FOUR: REALIZE THAT YOU HAVE AN OUTSIDE SOURCE OF STRENGTH.

Zacchaeus was encouraged to change because he knew now that he was not alone; he had an amazing out-side source of strength. Look what Jesus says at the end of the story: "Today salvation has come. . . . the Son of Man came to seek out and to save the lost" (verses 9-10).

One of my best friends is Dr. Don Webb. Don tells a personal story that is a wonderful parable. Don Webb was born in Wales, and he served in the Queen's Navy before coming to America to become a Methodist minister. He was so proud to be in the Royal Navy and was doubly proud when he was named captain of the H. M. S. Switha. He was the ship's captain, and he wanted so much to impress his crew. He wanted his men to know how wise and how brave their new captain was. One of their first assignments was to go out and check the anchors holding the buoys in place. The only way to do this was to send down a deep-sea diver. When they arrived at their first checkpoint, the first mate told Don Webb that his prede-cessor, their beloved former captain, always liked to go down first. Would he, as their new captain, like that privi-lege? Don Webb had never done any deep-sea diving. He had never worn a deep-sea diving suit. He didn't know the first thing about it; but unable to swallow his pride, unable to admit his inadequacy, unable to confess his need for help, Don Webb blurted out, "Of course I want to go down first. I wouldn't have it any other way!"

At this point in his story, Don went into a graphic description of putting on that heavy diving suit for the first time. He was scared to death but acting proud. He put on the leaded shoes, the heavy suit, the thick gloves. He described the locking on of the helmet, the closing of the window at the face of the helmet, the fear, the unfamiliar, eerie sounds, the claustrophobia, the queasiness. Next, he gave a detailed description of jumping overboard and going down to the ocean floor. At first, the water was beautiful, blue and clear . . . then greenish and then gray and then black. Then he told about hitting bottom and the heavy feet sinking deep into the mud. He felt so awkward, and it dawned upon him that he didn't know how to walk down there. He panicked and fell forward, face down in the mud, and as he fell he lost his lifeline. He remembered that his men had said to him earlier as they handed him his lifeline: "Whatever you do Cap'n, don't let go of this. If you need help, just give her a tug!"

Don described his plight. He had lost his lifeline. He was lying face down in the mud on the ocean floor. He was stuck and unable to move, and he was thinking, *This is it. This is how it all ends.* He lay there waiting to die, thinking, *Oh, my arrogant pride! How stupid of me!* After several minutes that seemed like an eternity, Don Webb felt a gentle touch on his shoulder. Help had come from above. The crew sensed that he had lost his lifeline, and they knew he was in trouble. One of the men who was an experienced diver had come down to save him, pick him up, get him unstuck from the mud, give back his lifeline, and show him how to walk and survive and how to do exciting, creative things down there on the ocean floor. Help had come from above to give him a new chance, a new beginning, a new life. Don was now ready to swallow his pride and confess his need for help. He had enough humility and trust to learn from an expert.

Isn't that a great parable for life? It's the Christ event, isn't it? You see, we have a great outside source of strength, help from above, a saving lifeline if we could only recognize it, if we could only swallow our pride and realize how much we need a Savior and how much he wants to help us. Zacchaeus saw it and felt it that day in Jericho. Christ came to him and changed his bad habits and changed his life. And do you know what? He wants to do that for you and me not just during the days of Lent this year, but forever.

Questions for Reflection and Discussion

1. What connections do you see between happiness and cultivating good habits? How do you respond to the

idea that we can find something happy even when a day is not good? Have you ever done this? What was it like? What thoughts or feelings did you have?

2. How do you define a bad habit? What bad habit would you like to give up? What might be different if you gave it up?

3. Prayerfully read Luke 19:1-10. How do you respond to the story of Zacchaeus and the changes in his life? How does the story challenge or inspire you as you think about giving up bad habits?

4. What value do you see in recognizing a bad habit and calling it by name?

5. What role does choice play in ending a bad habit? What feelings or thoughts do you have about making up one's mind to stop a bad habit right now? Do you think this choice is easy or difficult? Why?

6. How do you respond to the strategy and wisdom of replacing a bad habit with a good habit? When have you done this? What was it like?

7. How do you experience God's presence and power as you seek to eliminate bad habits?

Prayer

Dear God, thank you for the many good habits we have that outnumber our bad habits. Help us to replace the bad with the good. Encourage us and help us to take positive action to make a positive change in behavior. Give us patience to go forward and help us up when we fall. Show us that we can give up bad habits with your help. Amen.

Focus for the Week

This week, reflect on good and bad habits and their effects in your life. Consider ways to increase the good and decrease the bad. Take some small action steps to eliminate a bad habit. Ask God and others for help. Today is a new beginning.

1. From *Happiness is Sharing*, by J. Harvey Howells, edited by Maryjane Hooper Tonn (Ideals, 1977); page 32.
2. From the definition *publicans* in *Harper's Bible Dictionary*, edited by Paul J. Achtemeier (Society of Biblical Literature, 1985); page 841.

Give Up Pettiness for Lent

Scripture: Read Luke 6:32-36

S ome years ago, I heard a story of a highly respected minister in Louisiana named Dr. F. M. Freeman. Dr. Freeman served as pastor of some of the finest churches in the state and was greatly appreciated and deeply loved by both ministers and lay people. He was a delightful man known for his quick wit and his great sense of humor. When he was well up in his 80's, he had this conversation with a young minister one day: Dr. Freeman said, "I want to tell you something, and

I want you to remember this all of your life: never, never hate anybody!"

The young minister said, "I agree with you, Dr. Freeman. I agree with you completely."

Dr. Freeman said, "Now listen closely. Take this deep into your soul. I'm not saying this casually. I mean it with all my heart. Do not allow yourself to hate anyone. Life is too short for that!"

The young minister agreed with him again.

Then Dr. Freeman said, "Don't hate anyone. Life is too short. I have followed that advice all of my life." And then with a twinkle in his eye, Dr. Freeman patted his shirt pocket and said, "But I do carry this list around with me. If I ever backslide, I'll know right where I'm going to start!"

Now, of course, Dr. Freeman was just kidding around with that last comment. He understood that keeping such a list was petty. He knew that we often harbor feelings that are out of proportion to the events or circumstances that provoke them. Anyone who knew him found him to be a kind, loving, gracious person who did indeed understand that life is too short for hostility, hatred, vengeance, littleness, and grudges. He knew that such attitudes are spiritual poisons that will absolutely devastate our souls. Now, you and I know where he learned that, don't we? Of course we do! He learned it from Jesus.

Listen again to the words of Jesus in Luke 6:32-36: "If you love those who love you, what credit is that to you? For even sinners love those who love them. If you do good to those who do good to you, what credit is that to you? For even sinners do the same. . . . love your enemies, do good. . . . Your reward will be great, and you will be children of the Most High; for he is kind to the ungrateful and the wicked. Be merciful, just as your Father is merciful."

In this teaching from the Sermon on the Plain, Jesus was saying that life is too short for hatred and vengeance and grudges and malice and resentment and self-pity. We don't have to give in to those toxic attitudes. We don't have to live that way. With God as our helper, we can choose the way of love and grace and forgiveness. To choose this way of love is to move beyond pettiness into a more whole and healthy life.

Read this story I once heard: A woman went to her doctor one day with a catalog of complaints about her health. The physician examined her and became convinced that there was nothing physically wrong with her. He suspected that her problem was her negative outlook on life, her bitterness, her resentment, her grudges, her self-pity. Every day for her was a "woe-is-me pity party," another day to nurse her grievances, to feel sorry for herself and to become more and more angry over how, in her mind, she had been mistreated by people and by life in general.

The wise physician took her into a back room in his office where he kept some of his medicine. He showed her a shelf filled with empty bottles. He said to her, "See those bottles. Notice that they are all empty. They are shaped differently from one another, but basically they are all alike. Most importantly, they have nothing in them." He continued, "I can take one of these bottles and fill it with poison—enough poison to kill a human being. Or, I could take the same bottle and fill it with enough medicine to bring down a fever, ease a throbbing headache, or fight bacteria in the body. I make the choice. I can fill it with whatever I choose. I can fill it with poison that will hurt or with medicine that will heal."

Then, the doctor looked the woman straight in the eye and said, "Each day that God gives us is basically like one of these empty bottles. We can choose to fill it with love and life-affirming thoughts and attitudes that lift us and other people up, or we can fill it with destructive poisonous thoughts that pull us—and everyone we meet—down. The choice is ours."

The point of this story leads to a question: How will we fill our days? In Luke 6, Jesus gives us the answer. Let me paraphrase verses 35-36 for you. He says to spend our days imitating the gracious, loving, merciful, healing Spirit of God. In other words, "Life is too short for littleness and self-pity. Life is too short for hate and grudges and quarrelling. Life is

too short for resentment and jealousies. Life is too short
for anything less than love."

Let me spell this out a little further by listing some
ideas here that speak to us today as we concentrate on the
urgency and quickness of life. I offer three ideas. Life is too
short for pettiness, hurt feelings, and bitter ill will.

FIRST, LIFE IS TOO SHORT FOR PETTINESS.

We describe something that has little or no importance
as being petty. Negative feelings and ill will over circumstances that do not warrant them are what pettiness is
all about. Pettiness can cut us off from God, from other
people, and from the church.

I am thinking of a man I know in another state who is
a great singer. He has an outstanding tenor voice, but he
has not sung in church for more than twenty years. He was
active in his church's music program. He sang in the choir,
and he was the church's main soloist.

He went to a convention in New York and discovered
while he was there that some of the large churches in New
York City pay their choir members. When he returned
home, he gave his church an ultimatum. He said, "Pay
me, or I quit the choir!" The church declined his offer, and
he quit. The choir suffered his loss for a while, but soon
enough, others came along to take his place. None of us is
indispensable. The church rolls on.

But that man has sulked for over twenty years. He doesn't go to church much anymore, and when he does go, he sits in the congregation with bitterness written all over his face. He is mad most of the time. He is cynical and critical of the church, especially of the music program. People long ago stopped listening to his complaints. Now, here is a man who has wasted his talent. Think of what he has missed all those years while making himself miserable through pettiness! Life is too short for this. Pettiness is such a waste of time, talent, and energy.

SECOND, LIFE IS TOO SHORT FOR HURT FEELINGS.

Hurt feelings are often a signal of pettiness. I'm thinking of a woman who quite suddenly quit the church. When the pastor asked her why, she said, "My sister passed away on September 20, and I didn't get a sympathy card from my Sunday school class until October 3! I will never forgive the church or that class for slighting me like that!"

I wonder what Jesus would say to her. I wonder what the apostle Paul would say. My guess would be that they would say to her, "Come on now! Life is too short for that! Life is too short for pettiness and hurt feelings. They are such a waste."

THIRD, LIFE IS TOO SHORT FOR BITTER ILL WILL.

Pettiness can lead to bitterness and ill will that can contaminate your soul. I'm thinking of a couple who became upset with their church back in the early 1990's because of a decision the church made about a social issue. The couple became sick with bitterness and hostility. It was all they could talk about. At every meal, they fussed at the church. Each evening in the den, they harshly criticized the church and its leaders. They wrote angry, hot letters, complaining about the church. They looked constantly for materials to use against the church. They made abusive speeches blasting the church. This went on for five years, and their children looked on and listened and took it all in. Finally, their hostility spent, the couple decided to come back to the church. But they ran into something they hadn't counted on. Their children didn't want to have anything to do with the church now, and strangely, that couple couldn't understand why. For five years, they had bitterly denounced the church in front of their children because of one decision made by the administrative board. Inadvertently, they had taught their children to hate the church and its people.

Five years of bitterness. Five years of hostility. Five years of ill will. How do you undo the harm? How do you correct it? Is it too late? Life is too short for bitter ill will!

It is so dangerous and so harmful. It's a waste of time and energy, and in this case it had a negative effect on young lives.

Ill will is a phrase that refers to many things and covers a multitude of sins. Jealousy, envy, resentment, quarrelling, grudge-bearing, vengeance, stubborn pride, temper, haughtiness, spite, hatred, all of these are what we mean by *ill will*. Nothing is more spiritually draining.

Ill will is a fitting name for all of these attitudes because they are all sick! Christ came to bring wholeness, to make us well, to heal, to deliver us from all these sins of ill will. Isn't that what conversion is? Christ coming into our lives and changing our ill will to good will?

You may have heard the story of a lady who phoned her TV serviceman and complained that something was wrong with her television set. The serviceman asked her if there were any visible symptoms. "Well, the newscast is on right now," said the lady, "and the reporter has a very long face." The serviceman replied, "Lady, if you had to report what's happening these days, you'd have a long face too!" I know that many things in our world can drive us to ill will and a long face. I also know that a "faith adjustment" can make all the difference in how we view the world and in how we relate to it.

We only have so much energy, and broadly speaking, it can be used in one of two ways. We can use it for good or ill, to build up or tear down, to do the things of love, or to do the things of hate. Interestingly, both good will and ill will are like boomerangs. Whichever you send out will come back. If you give out love and good will, it comes back to bless you. If you give out hate and ill will, it comes back to haunt you.

The real truth is that life is just too short for bitter ill will. It's too short for grudges and quarrels and spites and prejudices and hates. In all of these attitudes of ill will, we cut ourselves off not only from people but also from God.

What about you? Are you letting some miserable, petty misunderstanding keep you constantly tense and spiritually drained? Are you feeling some jealousy or resentment? Are you keeping some quarrel alive? Are you holding a grudge? Do you need to say "I'm sorry" or "forgive me" or "I love you"? If so, now is the time to swallow your pride and set it right! Now is the time to do something about it! Don't let the sun go down tonight before you have fixed it. Tomorrow may be too late. Life passes so quickly. It is much too brief to give time and energy to littleness and pettiness. We were made in the image of God and meant to be big. Life is too short for anything less.

So, the point is clear: If we could—by the grace of God—give up pettiness for all of the days of Lent, then prayerfully, hopefully, we could—with God's help—give it up forever.

Questions for Reflection and Discussion

1. How do you define *pettiness*? What are some examples of attitudes that you would identify as petty?
   What can cause us to have these attitudes? What
   connection do you see between pettiness and more
   intense feelings such as hate?
2. Read Luke 6:32-36. What do these teachings say to
   you about pettiness?
3. What do you see as some of the many dangers of
   pettiness? What are some illustrations of ways that
   pettiness can affect our relationships with others?
   with God?
4. Why do you think hurt feelings can be harmful? In
   what ways can we minimize hurt feelings?
5. How do you respond to the statement that ill will
   spiritually drains us? What does being spiritually
   drained suggest to you?
6. How do you think God helps us eliminate pettiness
   and live bigger lives?

Prayer

Dear God, thank you for showing us that pettiness is
not an answer for a healthy and wholesome life. Thank
you for showing us a better way to live. Help us to be big
rather than small, generous rather than stingy. May we

strive to prevent hurt feelings in others and learn to share your love with all who are in our lives. Amen.

Focus for the Week

This week, practice being a generous and giving person. Overlook faults and slights. Avoid hurting the feelings of others. Use the Lenten season to make a positive change in how you look at and treat others. Focus on love and watch pettiness disappear.

Wrap Your Arms Around Something Good for Easter

Scripture: Read John 21:15-19

On November 1, 1972, our family left West Tennessee and moved to Shreveport, Louisiana, so I could join the staff of the First United Methodist Church there as the preaching associate. For the next twelve years, I had the distinct, unique, and amazing experience of working side-by-side daily with Dr. D. L. Dykes. Dr. Dykes was, without question, one of the greatest preachers I have ever heard, one of the most creative and innovative leaders I have ever known and one of the most lovingly colorful and eccentric personalities I have ever met. He was a legend in his own time. He had been on television in that area on the CBS-affiliate station for twenty years, and everybody in the Ark-La-Tex region of our country knew him. Everyone from the smallest child to the oldest adult affectionately called him "D. L."

D. L. was known far and wide for his driving. One time when I was in his car with him, the Shreveport police pulled us over. The patrolman walked up to the car, leaned over, looked in, and said, "Aw shucks, D. L. It's just you. Go on. I didn't recognize your new car."

The very first time I went anywhere with him in his car, he wanted to stop at the print shop in downtown Shreveport. When we got there, D.L. went around the block once and there were no parking places near the print shop. So he just jumped the curb, pulled up, and parked on the sidewalk in front of the print shop's main door! He jumped out, left the car engine running, asked me to stay there and watch the car, and then he ran into the print shop.

I was new to Shreveport, and I didn't know what to do except sit there and pray that the police wouldn't come by. I felt like the lookout in the get-away car. Well, before I could even get that prayer out, the police did come by. The policeman said, "Is this your car?" I said, "No, sir." "Whose car is it?" he asked. I said, "It belongs to Dr. D. L. Dykes." And the policeman asked, "This is D. L.'s car?"

"Yes, sir." "Well, O.K.," he said, "But tell him next time it would probably be best if he would park on the street." "Yes, sir," I said with a sigh of relief.

As well known as D. L. was for his driving, he was even more famous for his eloquent, powerful, conversational preaching. He never raised his voice. He just stood in the pulpit and talked in a conversational tone. He could hold a congregation in the palm of his hand because all of the people in the sanctuary and those watching on TV felt strongly that D. L. was speaking directly, personally, intimately, and individually to each one of them. D. L. was a fantastic storyteller and when he told a personal story about something that had happened to him in his early life, you were there with him. With his word, he could transport you back in time to that little house where he grew up in Pleasant Hill, Louisiana. The story would be so vivid, so powerful that you could smell the soup his mother was cooking in the kitchen!

As eloquent as D. L. was, one Sunday morning he got his tongue twisted and could not get out what he wanted to say. He was telling a story about a man he knew who had an interesting way of dealing with his problems. He would write his problems on a card on Friday afternoon and then place that card in a drawer in his desk. The man didn't want to take his problems home with him for the weekend. He didn't want his problems to be a burden to him and his family over the weekend, so he would leave the card with the problems written on it in a drawer in his desk. Then on the following Monday morning, he would take the card out and deal with the problems as best as he could.

That's what he meant to say, but on that fateful Sunday morning with 1,200 people in church and thousands more watching on television, here's what happened: He said, "I know this man who has a desk in his drawers. . . . " The congregation snickered at first and then laughed loudly. D. L. turned to me and said, "What did I say?" I answered, "You said you know a man who has a desk in his drawers." D. L. laughed and said, "That not what I meant to say. I meant to say, 'I know a man who has a desk in his drawers.' " The congregation roared again even more loudly. D. L. turned to me and said, "Did I do it again?" I said, "Yes, sir." He tried again and again and again—five times— and he never did get it right. Then, as only D. L. could do, he rose to the occasion and said, "Is there anybody here who has any idea what I'm trying to say?" And the congregation laughed again.

Now, the point is: It happens to the best of us. We can all get into trouble with our words. Sometimes we say the wrong things and our words come back to haunt us.

Have you heard about the mother who invited some people to dinner? At the table, she turned to her six-year-old daughter and said, "Would you like to say the blessing?"

The little girl replied, "I wouldn't know what to say." The mother insisted. "You can do it, honey. Just say what you hear Mommy say." The little girl bowed her head, closed her eyes, and said, "Lord, what on earth was I thinking when I invited all these people to dinner?"

This is what happened to Simon Peter on the night before Jesus was crucified. His words spoken in haste that fateful night in a moment of *braggadocio* came back to weigh heavily on his heart and thrust him into despair. Go back with me to that poignant scene.

Jesus and the disciples had just finished the Last Supper in the upper room. They sang a hymn and then went out to the Mount of Olives. There, Jesus told his disciples that they were fast approaching the "showdown," and in that crunch moment they would all fall away. They would all deny him, and they would all forsake Him. But boldly, Peter said to Jesus, "Not me, Lord. All the rest of them may fall away but not me. You can count on me. I would never fail you. I would never deny you. I will go with you to prison and even to death. The others may become weak in the crisis, but not me. I will stand tall. That, you can count on." And Jesus said, "Simon, Simon, I know you mean well, but the truth is that this very night before the cock crows, you will deny me three times" (John 13:37-38).

And, of course, Jesus was right. That is what happened, and Peter was emotionally and spiritually devastated by his failure to live up to his bold words. How could he face Christ again after falling on his face so completely? How could he be a trusted leader of the disciple group ever again after his colossal collapse? How could he speak ever again about his commitment to Christ and expect anybody to believe him? How could he redeem himself?

Well, the fact is, he couldn't redeem himself, but Christ could! The Risen Lord could redeem him and forgive him and encourage him and give him a new lease on life, and that is precisely what this wonderful story in John 21 is all about.

After the Crucifixion and the Resurrection, the Risen Lord comes looking for Simon Peter. He knows full well that Simon Peter had failed that night, not once, not twice, but three times. The Risen Christ knows how heartsick Simon Peter must be. He knows that Peter needs forgiveness, needs reassurance, needs a new chance, and a new life. So the Risen Christ comes to meet him where he is and to give him what he needs. This is the good news of Easter for you and me. This great story shows us that Christ not only can conquer evil and death, but also that he can resurrect us. He did that for Simon Peter that day. He can do it for you and me this day. That's what John 21 teaches us.

Who could ever forget that scene? After the Risen Christ serves the disciples breakfast (another Holy Communion), he looks Simon Peter square in the eye and asks

Peter the same question three times. "Simon, do you love me?" "Oh yes, Lord," Simon answers, "You know I love you." "Then, feed my sheep," the Risen Lord says to him. "Feed my sheep!" (John 21:15-18).

Of course, it's obvious what's going on here. Christ is forgiving Peter and giving him a chance to profess his love three times to make up for his earlier three-fold denial. Then the story ends exactly the way it started months before with Christ saying to Simon at the seashore these two powerful words: "Follow me." Notice this now: The first thing and the last thing Jesus said to Simon Peter was that simple command: "Follow me."

Isn't that a great story? It is jam-packed with the stuff of life, with powerful symbols, strong emotions, and dramatic lessons. One of the key lessons for us today is to see how the Risen Christ seeks out Simon Peter and meets his need and to see how he does that for us too. He seeks us out. He comes looking for us to meet our needs.

In Simon Peter's experience with Christ back then, we get a practical glimpse at three of the powerful ways the Risen Christ meets us and helps us today. Let me show you what I mean.

FIRST OF ALL, WHEN WE MOST NEED LOVE, THE RISEN CHRIST COMES TO LOVE US.

Perhaps you have heard this story: It was a busy morning in the doctor's office. Just a few minutes after eight, an elderly gentleman in his 80's showed up to have some stitches removed from his thumb. He told the nurse that he was in a big hurry because he had an important appointment at nine that morning, and he must not be late. The nurse took his vital signs and had him take a seat, knowing it would be over an hour before anyone would be able to see him. The nurse noticed that the man kept looking at his watch urgently, and she decided to see if she could help the man. She looked at his injured thumb, and it looked good. It was healing nicely. She reported this to the doctor, and he told her to go ahead and remove his stitches and to redress his thumb. As she was doing this, she and the older man got into a nice conversation.

"So you have an urgent appointment at 9:00 this morning?" she asked. "Yes," he said, "the same appointment I have every morning. Every morning at 9:00, I go to the nursing home to have breakfast with my wife." The nurse smiled and said, "You are such a handsome gentleman. I bet that's the highlight of her day." The man blinked and said, "She doesn't know who I am. She has had Alzheimer's disease for quite a while. She hasn't recognized me in the last five years." The nurse was surprised, and she said, "And you still go every morning, even though she doesn't know who you are?" The man smiled, patted the nurse's hand, and said, "She doesn't know who I am, but I know who she is."

There's a word for that. It's called *love*—unwavering, unshakable, unconditional love. And that's the kind of love Jesus Christ had for Simon Peter. He knew who Simon was, and he knew how Simon must have been feeling. He knew that Peter the Rock had crumbled and now felt like dirt! So here came the Risen Lord to give Simon Peter the encouragement, the affirmation, the reassurance, and the love he needed so much in that moment. No "I told you so" here. No stern lectures here. No fanning the flames of guilt here. No blame-placing or finger-pointing here. Just words of love.

In this powerful and touching breakfast scene, Jesus, the Risen Christ, is saying to Simon Peter: "I still love you. I still trust you. I still believe in you. I know you can do it. I want you to lead out. I want you to take up the torch of my ministry. I want you to take care of my sheep. I want you to watch over my flock."

Now, we know that these words of love became the wake-up call Simon Peter needed; and as we read on in the Scriptures, we see how he became one of the courageous leaders of the early church.

The point for us is obvious. Just as the Risen Christ came to Peter that day with the words and acts of love he so desperately needed, he comes to us with unwavering, unshakable, unconditional love. That's number one. When we most need love, the Risen Christ comes to love us.

SECOND, WHEN WE MOST NEED FORGIVENESS, THE RISEN CHRIST COMES TO FORGIVE US.

Simon Peter needed forgiveness and that is precisely what Christ came to give him.

It happened in the early 1970's. Her name was Teresa. She was sixteen years old and having a hard time growing up. One Friday night, she had an ugly fight with her parents. She ran away from home and stayed away for almost two years. Her parents searched desperately for her but with no luck. Finally, they hired a detective. The detective brought back a sordid story that I couldn't even begin to describe in the polite pulpit. Teresa had done everything a girl could do that would break her parents' hearts—drugs, alcohol, promiscuity. She participated in all kinds of illicit activity.

Then one morning (it was Good Friday), the phone rang in my office. It was a collect call from Teresa. She was calling from San Francisco. She was crying. "Oh, Jim," she said, "I have done everything wrong. I have hurt my parents so much. Now I realize how foolish I have been. I want to come home, but I don't know if Mom and Dad want me back. I wouldn't blame them if they didn't. I don't know how they could ever forgive me. I'm so sorry, and I want to come home." I told her to go to the airport and give her name at the airline desk. I would have a ticket home waiting there for her, and someone would be at the local airport to meet her plane.

When she got off the plane on that Good Friday afternoon, she looked pretty rough. Her hair was dirty and matted. Her clothes were rumpled and threadbare. Her eyes were tired and bloodshot. Her parents rushed to her and hugged her and welcomed her home with love and grace. They were crying tears of joy and relief.

Two days later on Easter Sunday morning, they were in church together. Teresa sat between her mom and dad. She looked like a new person. She was radiant and beautiful. All through the service, her parents kept touching her, patting her, hugging her. After the service, they came down to speak to me. As Teresa's mother hugged me tightly, she whispered in my ear, "Jim, I've always believed in the Resurrection but never more than right now!"

Through the power of God's amazing grace, we can work miracles when we, in the spirit of the Risen Christ, reach out to others with forgiveness. When we need it most, the Risen Christ comes looking for us with love and forgiveness.

FINALLY, WHEN WE MOST NEED DIRECTION, THE RISEN CHRIST COMES TO DIRECT US.

Simon Peter and the other disciples had been waiting around wondering, *What next? What are we supposed to do now?* Then the Risen Christ came to give them a new direction. He said to Peter, "If you love me, then feed my sheep." What he meant was, "Take up the torch of my ministry! Go! Be the church for this needy world!" The world is starving to death for Jesus Christ and we have him. Our task is to feed his sheep, to share him with others (verses 15-19).

I have a good friend who is one of the most outgoing, gregarious persons I have ever known. He is so full of life that he just lights up the room. Physically, he is a great big guy—a former football player, strong and powerful—and yet he has a teddy-bear personality. He is a hugger. He hugs everybody; he is wired up that way. He expresses his love with hugs.

Some years ago, I heard him speak to a group of young people, and he said something that inspired them and touched me. He said, "When I first became a Christian, I was so frustrated because I wanted to hug God and didn't know how." He said, "I was so thrilled by what God had done for me in Christ. I was so grateful for the way God had turned my life around, I wanted to hug God, but I didn't know how." And then he said this: "Over the years,

I have learned that the best way to hug God is to hug his children. The best way to love God is to love his children. The best way to serve God is to serve his children."

He's right, you know. That's precisely what the Risen Christ was saying to Peter that day. "If you love me, then feed my sheep, take care of my flock. That's the direction I want you to take. That's exactly what I want you to do."

Now, let me tell you something. The Risen Christ is here with us today. He is here right now. He has come to give us the love, the forgiveness, and the direction we so desperately need.

Questions for Reflection and Discussion

1. What does the idea of embracing something good for Easter suggest to you?
2. Prayerfully read John 21:15-19. How do you respond to the interactions between Jesus and Peter? What stands out most for you?
3. What are some of the ways the Risen Christ comes to love you when you need it the most?
4. When have you experienced forgiveness? When have you forgiven someone else? How was God present for you?
5. When have you experienced God's guidance as you sought direction in your life? What was it like?

6. What does *resurrection* mean to you? How do you think resurrection happens to us?

Prayer

Dear God, thank you for this experience and opening our eyes to all the possibilities of Lent and Easter. Help us to go forward from here making changes to our lives and changing the lives of others in the progress. Encourage us to recognize and embrace the good in Easter and to celebrate our Risen Lord every day. Amen.

Focus for the Week

Consider what you have learned and how you have grown from this Lenten experience and implement the changes you want to make in your life. Celebrate the season by showing God's love to others and becoming the person God wants you to be.

Made in the USA
Middletown, DE
11 February 2023

24631215R00057